Integrating GIS Technologies with the Visual Resource Management Inventory Process

Technical Note 407

By:

Russell Jackson
Cartographer
Branch of Photogrammetric
Applications
BLM National Science
and Technology Center
Denver, Colorado

Chris Horyza
Planning Team
Leader/GIS Specialist
BLM Phoenix Field Office
Phoenix, Arizona

November 2001

U.S. Department of the Interior
Bureau of Land Management

Suggested citation:

Jackson, R. and C. Horyza. 2001. Integrating GIS technologies with the visual resource management inventory process, Technical Note 407. Bureau of Land Management, Denver, Colorado. BLM/WO/ST-01/001+8400. 27 pp.

Table of Contents

Introduction

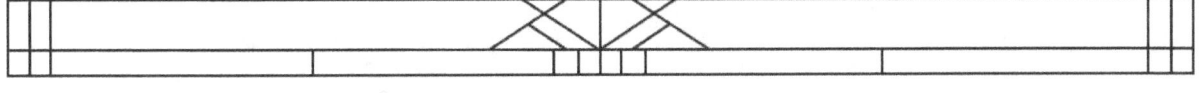

The purpose of this technical note is to assist field offices in using current geographic information systems (GIS) and image processing technologies to facilitate new, or improve on existing, visual resource management (VRM) inventories. This technical note seeks to use technology available in the field to improve existing VRM inventory procedures without changing the basic concepts the inventory is built on.

As previously noted in WO IM No. 2001-038, Development/Approval of Preparation Plans for New Planning Starts, use of current technologies are needed to assist managers in completing new, or amending current, planning documents. The methodology described throughout this technical note can be quickly distributed to the field and provides defensible and repeatable VRM data for inclusion in the Bureau's resource management plan (RMP) process.

This technical note attempts to modernize the VRM inventory process by taking advantage of advances in GIS and image processing technologies in order to accomplish the following goals:

- Enhance the repeatability of VRM results.
- Reduce the amount of time needed to conduct an inventory.
- Reduce the workload that a VRM inventory has on the local office.

- Reduce the cost of the inventory.
- Improve the quality of VRM inventories for land management decisionmakers.

Inventory Process Model

The inventory process model described here represents a process guided primarily by a traditional VRM inventory using GIS as a storage and production medium. This model requires:

- Simple overlay analysis and reporting. Most of the analysis and reporting would require only basic training in GIS applications. The training could be provided by a State Office, the National Science and Technology Center (NSTC), or contract experts on a periodic or "as needed" basis.

- Local inventory labor. This process model generally provides a combination of technical expertise and labor requirements within the capacity of most field offices.

- Data preparation. This would be necessary prior to any GIS analysis being performed. If possible, this could be accomplished by the current field office staff. The data preparation could be provided by a State Office, the NSTC, or contract experts on a periodic or "as needed" basis.

- Local GIS support. The support could be provided by resource specialists with GIS ability or "as-needed" off-site support. Regardless of how the GIS support is acquired, it is recommended that a GIS Specialist be an active member of the interdisciplinary team performing the scenic evaluations.

Assumptions

Three assumptions guided development of this inventory process model:

- The VRM inventory process is followed as described in BLM Manual Handbook 8410-1, *Visual Resource Inventory*. It may be argued that some adjustments to the VRM inventory procedure are made with each inventory. Handbook H 8410-1, Section I, Implementation Options, states that adaptations to the inventory method may be made if they (1) provide a more cost-effective way to complete a quality inventory, and (2) keep the conceptual framework of VRM system intact. It is believed the inventory process model described here meets these criteria.

- The data generated in support of local VRM inventories will conform to the BLM Standard Theme Specifications for the Visual Resource Management Program (see Appendix A).

- The spatial component of any data generated during the VRM process will meet the guidelines for geospatial data at a scale of 1:100,000, as stipulated by the Federal Geographic Data Committee (FGDC), Geospatial Positioning Accuracy Standards, Part 3: National Standard for Spatial Data Accuracy. See the FGDC's Web site (*www.fgdc.gov*) for complete details.

Determining Key Observation Points and Minimum Mapping Units

Before any major analysis or mapping for the VRM inventory can be completed, two decisions must be made:

- What are the visual resource management objectives of the inventory and how will these objectives be expressed by the selection of key observation points (KOPs) or areas? Much of the analysis and mapping will be based on the locations of these KOPs and they should be selected at the beginning of the process. How this selection is made may vary from inventory to inventory.

- What is the minimum mapping unit (MMU) that will be used? The MMU is used to express what the smallest manageable VRM unit can be. It can vary from less than 100 to several thousand acres. This is important because a GIS can generate a large number of very small areas (or polygons or pixels) that, in a practical sense, are not manageable. By deciding at the beginning of the project what the minimum size area that is practical to manage will be, techniques in GIS can be used to keep the product maps as simple as possible and yet reflect realistic management objectives.

These two decisions should be based on the unique physiographic characteristics of the inventory area and the objectives driving the management of the visual resources. Since these decisions will vary from office to office, and possibly between inventories within offices, inventories conducted by different offices, or by different teams at different times, may not seamlessly fit together into a map representing a larger area.

Data Categories

Information, or data, that must be addressed during the VRM inventory process can be divided into three main categories: data identification, data conversion, and data analysis.

Data Identification

Data identification includes data that needs to be identified, or acquired, by the VRM team prior to beginning the VRM inventory. Some examples are:

- Location of key observation points (KOPs) on overlays
- Highlighting vegetation communities and their characteristics on overlays
- Location of existing structures in the visible landscape and their proper placement on an overlay
- Acquisition of digital elevation models

Data Conversion

Data conversion refers to the type of information that may be created prior to GIS analysis being performed. Some examples are:

- Digitizing or scanning of overlays
- Registration of those same overlays
- Projection or reprojection of data

Data Analysis

Data analysis refers to the variety of GIS data that will be generated while performing the VRM inventory. Some examples are:

- Buffers at various distances
- Viewshed analysis for visible or not visible (one example is to identify seldom seen areas)
- Conversion of polygon data to grids and adding multiple grids together
- Conversion of grids back to polygons (conversion to shape files)
- Overlay (intersection or clip) to assess acreage
- Production of map products for field or office use.

The examples provided for each of the categories are not all inclusive and should not be treated as such. They are provided for guidance and to show the types of data that may be needed by the VRM team. Specific data needs will vary from team to team and from inventory to inventory.

Steps within data conversion and data analysis may require the conversion of hardcopy plots or maps to digital format by digitizing, scanning, or some form of grid conversion. Digitizing could be performed on a variety of tablets found around the agency. Grid conversion can be performed within a number of GIS applications. While the GIS application used is not critical for digitizing or grid conversion, the Bureau's default application at the time this publication went to press was ESRI's Arc/Info. ESRI provides an excellent suite of software products that will perform conversions as well as meet all the needs of the inventory teams. However, other GIS applications are capable of providing the same functionality as Arc/Info. Regardless of the application used, be sure that data formats and structures are consistent and that the application provides portability between systems via some type of exchange format.

VRM Inventory Components

There are three primary components to consider in completing a VRM inventory: a scenic quality evaluation, a sensitivity level analysis, and a delineation of distance zones. Following is a discussion of these three components and recommendations on how to complete them utilizing GIS and image processing technologies.

Scenic Quality Evaluation— Key Factors

The scenic quality evaluation component of the VRM inventory is divided into seven key factors: landform, vegetation, water, color, scarcity, cultural modifications, and adjacent scenery. Each of the factors is rated separately, allowing the combination of factors to define the boundaries of differing scenic quality rating units (SQRUs). Though the handbook calls for defining SQRUs before rating the evaluation factors, even in its most rudimentary application, GIS can assist with the complex overlay analysis required to allow the landscape to define the units. Each rating factor and the proposed solution will be discussed. The explanations of the rating criteria for the key factors have been adapted from BLM Handbook 8410-1.

During the discussion of the seven key factors, certain aspects will appear very similar and repetitive from key factor to key factor. Yet, because the key factors are so very distinctive they must be addressed and completed individually. In fact, the data capture phase is extremely critical to the success of the entire VRM inventory process. Without proper data input, the process potentially could be completed but generate invalid results. To ensure this doesn't happen, a methodical and conscientious approach when capturing the initial data is critical. Be sure the spatial data corresponds to the numerical rating generated from H-8410-1, Scenic Quality Inventory and Evaluation Chart, Illustration 2 (see Appendix B).

Landform

The rating criteria for landform is that topography becomes more interesting as it gets steeper or more massive, or more severely or universally sculptured.

The team evaluating the inventory area would map areas according to their landform rating as described on the Scenic Quality Inventory and Evaluation Chart. Mapping would be done at 1:100,000 scale, or larger, as appropriate to the inventory area.

Mylar overlays would be placed over the maps. Using their knowledge of the area being evaluated, team members would annotate areas of particular landform interest on the overlays. The overlays would then be digitized or scanned and converted to grid (cell or raster) data for later analysis.

Vegetation

The rating criteria for vegetation gives primary consideration to the variety of patterns, forms, and textures created by plant life.

Vegetation is classified as described in the traditional inventory method on the Scenic Quality Inventory and Evaluation Chart and mapped on 1:100,000 scale overlays (or a scale appropriate to the inventory area). As with the discussion under landform, mylar overlays should be used by the team to capture the appropriate vegetation information. The overlays are then digitized and converted to grid for later analysis.

Water

The rating criteria for water describes it as that ingredient which adds movement or serenity to a scene; the degree to which water dominates the scene is the primary consideration in selecting the rating score.

Manual mapping of areas is rated for the dominance of visible water's contribution to the scene as described. This is mapped on a 1:100,000 scale, then digitized and converted to grid for later analysis.

Color

The rating criteria for color considers the overall color(s) of the basic components of the landscape (e.g., soil, rock, vegetation) as they appear during seasons or periods of high use. Criteria to use when rating color can be described in the context of variety, contrast, and harmony.

Based on the knowledge of the team and field visits as necessary, map areas of rich color

contrasts and variety and rate them as described on the Scenic Quality Inventory and Evaluation Chart. This is mapped on a 1:100,000 scale, then digitized and converted to grid for later analysis.

Scarcity

The rating criteria for scarcity provides an opportunity to give added importance to one or all of the scenic features that appear to be relatively unique or rare. Rating scores are based on the degree of the feature's rarity and on the opportunity for consistent exceptional wildlife or wildflower viewing. This key factor allows a rating score over five with a written justification.

Landscape features that are unique or rare in the physiographic region are mapped and rated according to the criteria in the Scenic Quality Inventory and Evaluation Chart. These overlays are then digitized and converted to grid for later analysis.

Cultural Modifications

The rating criteria explains that cultural modifications in the landform/water, vegetation, and addition of structures should be considered and may detract from the scenery in the form of a negative intrusion or complement or improve the scenic quality of a landscape. This is the only scenic quality key factor that can receive a negative score, reducing the overall scenic rating.

Existing cultural modifications can be mapped in the "visible" area. Based on local knowledge and field visits where considered necessary, landscapes can be mapped and rated according to the visual impact of those features. These overlays would be digitized and converted to grid for later analysis.

Adjacent Scenery

The rating criteria describes adjacent scenery as the degree to which scenery outside the scenery unit being rated enhances the overall impression of the scenery within the rating unit. This factor is generally applied to units that would normally rate very low in score, but the influence of the adjacent unit would enhance the visual quality and raise the score.

In a practical sense, if the adjacent scenery key factor can add from 0 to 5 points to a scenic quality rating, then the preliminary scenic quality rating score must be between 7 and 11 for this factor to have an effect on the overall rating. Regardless of the analytical model, the scores for the other scenic quality key factors should be added together first. If the total score for scenic quality is between 7 and 11, only then should the adjacent scenery key factor be analyzed, scored, and added to the scenic quality total score.

For those areas determined to have a preliminary scenic quality rating of C, but are close enough to the B rating to potentially benefit from an adjacent scenery score, the team can adjust the scenic quality rating based on consensus of the influence of adjacent scenery. This is a subjective rating and adjustments to the GIS database would be done manually.

Scenic Quality Evaluation Methodology

The proposed scenic quality evaluation methodology is divided into the following steps:

1. All grids that were created representing the scenic quality key factors are mathematically added together.

2. The product grid can be reclassified into three categories based on the scenic quality rating guidance in handbook H-8410-1, where scores of 11 or less = C scenery, 12 to 18 = B scenery, and 19 or more = A scenery.

3. Areas with scores of 7 to 11 can be extracted separately for consideration of the adjacent scenery key factor.

4. Once a final scenic quality rating grid is generated, it is vectorized and any polygons smaller than the agreed upon MMU absorbed (eliminated) into the larger surrounding units.

An alternative to vectorizing the grid data would be to analyze for clumps of grid cells of similar value that total less than the agreed upon MMU size and absorb them into the majority surrounding rating unit.

This small area elimination process could wait until the final VRM inventory classification is complete, but may keep the overall process cleaner if it is done at this point. Regardless of when it is done, a grid should be the product of the scenic quality evaluation and it should be available for later analysis with the other major VRM components.

Sensitivity Level Analysis

The ratings for evaluating scenic sensitivity are, by design, very subjective. This component of the VRM inventory is the public's opportunity to have their feelings and opinions about areas in the landscape addressed in the ranking process. Because of this subjectivity, there could be tremendous variability in the ratings generated by adjoining offices, and GIS support of the process could be potentially complex. Therefore, this process defers to traditional methods of acquiring this information.

Sensitivity Level Rating Units

Using traditional techniques to assess visual sensitivity, delineate sensitivity level rating units (as described in handbook H-8410-1 at 1:100,000 scale) and score their sensitivity. Digitize these overlays and convert to grid for later analysis with the other two VRM inventory component overlays.

Distance Zones

The basic assumption of distance analysis is that visual change is more significant the closer it is to the observer. In the traditional approach to this VRM component, KOPs or areas are defined at the beginning of the inventory and this component is analyzed from those.

Use of GIS technology can result in considerable savings of time and a more accurate representation of the visible landscapes from pre-mapped KOPs and areas. The result of this analysis, if documented, is also more repeatable and defensible than the traditional method.

Handbook H-8410-1 defines two distance-related zones and one zone related to landscape screening for this component.

Foreground/ . . . . 0–5 miles from KOP
Middleground

Background . . . . 5–15 miles from KOP

Seldom Seen . . . . Areas screened from view or
7–15 miles from KOP

GIS definition of these zones will require several steps.

The recommended methodology for computing distance zones is divided into the following steps:

1. Define and map the KOPs on 1:100,000 map overlays and digitize them.

2. Generate distance buffers from the KOPs consistent with the distances defined in H-8410-1 for the foreground/middleground and background zones. To the product map, add an attribute called "value" and assign 5 to foreground/middleground and 15 to background.

3. Conduct a viewshed analysis from the same KOP data using medium resolution terrain data (30-90 meter). The pixels that are classified as not seen are extracted to a new layer and assigned a value of 1. This represents the seldom-seen class.

4. The products of steps 2 and 3 are combined in a way that where the seldom seen exists, it replaces the distance zone pixels. (Merge or mosaic can be used, but be aware of the consequences on the outcome of the order in which maps are specified.)

5. Areas smaller than the agreed upon MMU should be absorbed into the larger classes surrounding them. The final product will be a raster layer with all three zones represented.

Visual Resource Inventory Classes

The process of defining the visual resource inventory classes is the same regardless of the office performing the inventory. Using raster processing capability, the overlays for the three components (and special management areas if there are any) are added together or recombined for the final classes. Two possible methods are provided.

Method 1

1> Assign the value of 1000 to all features of the Special Management Areas (Wilderness) overlay.
2> Assign values to the Scenic Quality where "A" scenery = 500, "B" scenery = 300, and "C" scenery = 100.
3> Assign values to Visual Sensitivity where High = 50, Moderate = 30, and Low = 10.
4> Assign values to the Distance Zones where foreground/middle ground = 5, Background = 3, and Seldom Seen = 1.

Then, add the reclassified raster maps together and reclassify the product as follows:

1> Values greater than or equal to 1000 = Class I.
2> Values greater than or equal to 355 but less than 1000 = Class II.
3> Values of 155, 335, and 353 = Class III.
4> The value of 351 is Class III if it is adjacent to Class III, II, or I. If adjacent to Class IV, it is Class IV.
5> All other values = Class IV.

Method 2

If the GIS supports Boolean analysis, the cell values are not as important as in Method 1, as long as they can be defined by their appropriate class. A Boolean formula, such as follows, could be written to define the visual resource inventory classes from the separate overlays.

If Special Management Areas = yes, Class I.

Or, if Scenic Quality is "A", Class II,

Or, if Scenic Quality is "B," and Sensitivity is "high," and Distance is "foreground/middle ground", Class II,

Or, if Scenic Quality is "B," and Sensitivity is "high," and Distance is "background," Class III,

Or, if Scenic Quality is "B," and Sensitivity is "medium," and Distance is "foreground/middle ground," Class III,

Or, if Scenic Quality is "B," and Sensitivity is "high," and Distance is "seldom seen,' and adjacent to Class I, II, or III, Class III,

Or, if Scenic Quality is "B," and Sensitivity is "high," and Distance is "seldom seen,' and adjacent to Class IV, Class IV,

Or, if Scenic Quality is "C," and Sensitivity is "high," and Distance is "foreground/middle ground," Class III,

Or, if Scenic Quality is "B," and Sensitivity is "medium," and Distance is "background" or "seldom seen," Class IV,

Or, if Scenic Quality is "B," and Sensitivity is "low," Class IV,

Or, if Scenic Quality is "C," and Sensitivity is "high," and Distance is "background" or "seldom seen," Class IV,

Or, if Scenic Quality is "C," and Sensitivity is "medium" or "low," Class IV.

The previous classification methods are just two possibilities. Both were based on the table in handbook H-8410-1, Illustration 11, under section A2 (see Appendix C). These analyses simply use the same products described in the handbook, but derived from various digital methods. The classification criteria used to derive the final inventory classes is the same. The crosshatching patterns described in section B of the same illustration, though elegant in their simplicity as a method to derive VRM classes, would be unnecessary.

Visual Resource Management Classes

At this point in the process, the product map represents the visual resource inventory classes. Conversion of these to final visual resource management classes involves assessment by the public, the planning team, and management as a part of the alternative and impact assessment in the resource management plan/environmental impact statement (RMP/EIS) process. Changes may be made to the classes or their boundaries to conform to the management objectives defined in the RMP/EIS. These changes may take the form of manual manipulation of the data or can be generated from other GIS analysis. The changes made and methods used will be unique to each RMP/EIS. The final product of this effort will be the visual resource management classes data.

Bibliography

Publications

Ackerson, V. and E. Fish. 1980. "An Evaluation of Landscape Units," Photogrammetric Engineering and Remote Sensing, Vol 46, No.3, pp. 347 358.

Carlson, C. and G. Jones. 1996. Evaluating scenic resources. Technical Information Series, Vol. 3, No. 1, Scenic America.

Galliano, S. and G. Loeffler. 2000. Scenery assessment: scenic beauty at the ecoregion scale. Gen. Tech. Rep. PNW-GTR-472. USDA Forest Service.

Hanna, K. 1999. GIS for landscape architects. ESRI Press. Redlands, CA.

Hanna, K. and R. Brian Culpepper. 1998. GIS in site design. John Wiley & Sons, Inc., New York, NY.

Litton Jr., R. Burton and Tetlow, Robert. 1978. A landscape inventory framework: scenic analyses of the northern Great Plains. PSW-135. USDA Forest Service Research Paper.

Magill, A. 1992. Managed and natural landscapes: what do people like? PSW 213. Pacific Southwest Research Station, USDA Forest Service.

Magill, A. 1990. Assessing public concern for landscape quality: a potential model to identify visual thresholds. PSW-203. Pacific Southwest Research Station, USDA Forest Service.

McGaughey, R. and A. Ager. 1996. UTOOLS and UVIEW: analysis and visualization software.

Miller, P. 1984. A comparative study of the BLM scenic quality rating procedure and landscape preference dimensions. Landscape Journal, Vol. 3, No. 2.

Sempek, J. 1991. VRMS/MOSS-MAPS pilot study, Cedar City District, Kanab Resource Area, Utah. USDI Bureau of Land Management.

Sipes, J, 1998. Shaping digital terrain. Landscape Architecture Magazine.

U.S. Department of Agriculture. Forest Service. 1996. Landscape aesthetics: a handbook for scenery management. USDA Forest Service Handbook Number 701.

U.S. Department of Agriculture, Forest Service. 1971. Inventorying and quantifying the visual resource. 2380 Landscape Management. USDA Forest Service, Region 1, Missoula, MT.

U.S. Department of Agriculture, Forest Service. 1997. Scenery management system using geographic information systems. Cibola National Forest, R3, USDA Forest Service.

U.S. Department of the Interior, Bureau of Land Management. 1984. Visual resource management. BLM Manual Handbook H-8400, Rel. 8-24. Washington, DC.

U.S. Department of the Interior, Bureau of Land Management. 1986. Visual resource inventory. BLM Manual Handbook H-8410-1, Rel. 8-28. Washington, DC.

U.S. Department of the Interior, Bureau of Land Management. 1986.Visual resource contrast rating. BLM Manual Handbook H-8431-1, Rel. 8-30. Washington, DC.

Web Sites

3DNature, Inc., World Construction Set. <www.3dnature.com> (March 2001)

American Society of Landscape Architects. <http://www.asla.org> (February 2001)

Buckley, D., C. Ulbricht, and J. Berry. 1998. The virtual forest: Advanced 3-D visualization techniques for forest management and research. GIS-98 @ Resource Technology Conference. <http://www.innovativegis.com/products/vforest> (November 2000)

Bureau of Land Management, Visual Resource Management. <http://www.blm.gov/nstc/VRM/index.html> (February 2001)

Computers & Geosciences. <http://www.elsevier.com> (October 2000)

ESRI. ArcView 3D Analyst Tutorial. Redlands, California. <www.esri.com> (March 2001)

ESRI. ArcView Spatial Analyst Tutorial. Redlands, California. <www.esri.com> (March 2001)

IEEE Technical Committee on Visualization and Graphics. <http://www.cc.gatech.edu/gvu/tccg/> (February 2001)

Imaging Systems Laboratory, Department of Landscape Architecture, Pennsylvania State University. <www.imlab.psu.edu/projects/index.html> (November 2001)

Landscape Architecture & Environmental Planning, University of California. <http://www-laep.ced.berkeley.edu/laep/index.html> (December 2000)

Open GL Organization. <www.opengl.org> (February 2001)

Orland, B., E. Weidemann, L. Larsen, and P. Radja. 1997. Exploring the relationship between visual complexity and perceived beauty. University of Illinois. <http://www.landarch.uiuc.edu> (November 2001)

MacEechren, A. and J.M.Kraak. Proposed terms of reference 1993 @ 2003. International Cartographic Association Commission on Visualization & Virtual Environments. <http://www.geovista.psu.edu/index.html> (November 2000)

Pennsylvania State University, Geographic Visualization Science, Technology, and Applications Center. <http://www.geovista.psu.edu/index.html> (November 2000)

USDA Forest Service. 1998. Vantage point, image and paper collection. University of Washington and the USDA Forest Service, Pacific Northwest Research Station. <http://forsys.cfr.washington.edu> (November 2000)

Appendix A

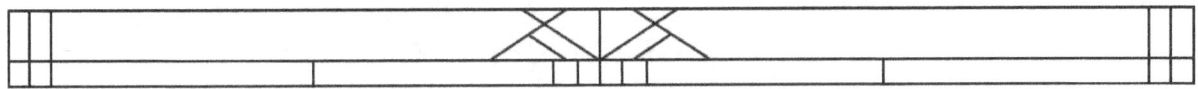

BUREAU OF LAND MANAGEMENT
STANDARD THEME SPECIFICATIONS
FOR THE VISUAL RESOURCE MANAGEMENT PROGRAM

THEME NAME: Scenic Quality Class

THEME ABBREVIATION: vr.sqc

PURPOSE: This theme identifies visual resource considerations that must be made in resource management plans (RMPs) and in the implementation of resource projects.

DESCRIPTION: This theme identifies the scenic quality of the landscape, which is an inventory component of BLM's Visual Resource Management System. Scenic Quality is the overall impression retained after driving through, walking through, or flying over an area of land. Each area is rated by seven factors: landform, vegetation, water, color, influence of adjacent scenery, scarcity, and cultural modifications.

SOURCE: Information is based on field examination and professional judgement regarding scenic values. This information may be documented in a separate report available from previous work (done by contract or by BLM) or it may be created or updated as part of an ongoing planning activity. It must be incorporated (in full or by reference) in the management situation analysis (MSA) document for each RMP.

DATA FEATURE TYPE: Polygon

THEME TYPE: Basic

HISTORICAL RECORD: Yes

UNIQUE IDENTIFIER: Identify by State/Field Office/polygon number. For example, ut050.010 means Utah/Richfield Field Office/polygon #10.

SCALE: 1:100,000

ATTRIBUTE DEFINITIONS:
Class A: These areas combine the most outstanding characteristics of each rating factor.

Class B: These areas have a combination of some outstanding features and some that are fairly common to the physiographic region.

Class C: These areas have only features that are common to the physiographic region.

THEME NAME: Visual Sensitivity

THEME ABBREVIATIONS: vr.vs

PURPOSE: Visual resource considerations must be made in resource management plan (RMP) decisions and in the implementation of resource projects.

DESCRIPTION: Visual sensitivity is an inventory component of BLM's Visual Resource Management System.

SOURCE: This information is obtained from field studies, visitor use or traffic statistics, and is documented in the management situation analysis (MSA) of RMPs.

DATA FEATURE TYPE: Polygon

THEME TYPE: Basic

HISTORICAL RECORD: Yes

UNIQUE IDENTIFIER: Identify by state/Field Office/polygon number. For example, ut050.001 means Utah/Richfield Field Office/polygon #1.

SCALE: 1:100,000

ATTRIBUTES:	CODES:
High Sensitivity	H
Medium Sensitivity	M
Low Sensitivity	L

ATTRIBUTE DEFINITIONS:

Visual sensitivity is the measure of human attitudes in the evaluation of a landscape. Visual sensitivity is determined in two ways: 1) use volume and 2) user or public reaction. The two ratings are combined in a matrix to determine the overall sensitivity rating of high, medium, or low.

THEME NAME: Visual Distance Zones

THEME ABBREVIATIONS: vr.vdz

PURPOSE: Visual resource considerations must be made in resource management plans (RMSs), in the implementation of projects, and in management actions.

DESCRIPTION: Visual distance zones are inventory components of BLM's Visual Resource Management System. Distance zones provide consideration of the proximity of the observer to the landscape. The quality of a landscape (and reaction) may be magnified or diminished by the visibility of the landscape from major viewing routes and key observation points. A landscape scene can be divided into three basic distance zones: foreground/middleground, background, and seldom seen.

SOURCE: This information can be determined from topographic information and field observation. It is usually part of an overall visual resource investigation and is documented along with the other portions of the study, in a separate report in the management situation analysis (MSA) for an RMP. In some cases this theme can be generated by computer program if suitable topographic information and key observation points or routes are available in the data base.

DATA FEATURE TYPE: Polygon

THEME TYPE: Basic and Generated

HISTORICAL RECORD: Yes

UNIQUE IDENTIFIER: Identify by State/Field Office/polygon number. For example, ut050.008 means Utah/Richfield Field Office/polygon #8.

SCALE: 1:100,000

ATTRIBUTES: **CODES:**

Foreground/	
Middleground Zone	FM
Background Zone	BG
Seldom Seen Zone	SS

ATTRIBUTE DEFINITIONS:

Foreground/Middleground Zone: This is the area that can be seen from each travel route or sensitivity area for a distance of 3 to 5 miles where management activities might be viewed in detail.

Background: This is the remaining area that can be seen from each travel route to approximately 15 miles.

Seldom Seen: This is the area that is not visible from each travel route or sensitivity area or is the area visible beyond approximately 15 miles. Because areas that are closer have a greater effect on the observer, such areas require more attention than do areas that are farther away.

THEME NAME: Visual Resource Management Inventory Classes

THEME ABBREVIATION: vr.vrmic

PURPOSE: Visual resource considerations must be made in resource management plans (RMPs) and in the implementation of resource projects. Although this theme provides generated information, it is given its own theme for data storage purposes and ease of retrieval.

DESCRIPTION: Visual resource management (VRM) inventory classes are inventory components of BLM's Visual Resource Management Program. They result from combining the other VRM inventory components including distance zones, sensitivity levels, and scenic quality.

SOURCE: This theme is derived by combining the vr.vdz,vr.vs, and vr.sqc themes.

DATA FEATURE TYPE: Polygon

THEME TYPE: Generated

HISTORIC RECORD: Yes

UNIQUE IDENTIFIER: Identify by State/Field Office/polygon number. For example, ut050.010 means Utah/Richfield Field Office/polygon #10

SCALE: 1:100,000

ATTRIBUTES: **CODES:**

VRM Inventory Class I	I
VRM Inventory Class II	II
VRM Inventory Class III	III
VRM Inventory Class IV	IV

ATTRIBUTE DEFINITIONS:

VRM Inventory Class I areas are where only natural ecological changes and very limited management activities occur. Any contrast created within the characteristic landscape must not attract attention. This classification is applied to wilderness areas, visual ACEC's, key natural areas bordering scenic travel routes, and other similar situations.

VRM Inventory Class II areas are where changes in any of the basic elements (form, line, color, texture) caused by a surface-disturbing activity should not be evident in the characteristic landscape. Contrasts must not attract attention.

VRM Inventory Class III areas are where contrasts to the basic elements caused by a management activity may be evident, but should remain subordinated to the natural landscape.

VRM Inventory Class IV areas are where contrasts may attract attention and be a dominant feature of the landscape in terms of scale, but should repeat the form, line, color and texture of the characteristic landscape.

THEME NAME: Visual Resource Management Classes

PURPOSE: Visual resource considerations must be made in resource management plans (RMP's), in the implementation of projects, and in management actions.

DESCRIPTION: Each of the four Visual Resource Management (VRM) Classes allows for a different degree of modification to the basic elements of the landscape. VRM classes are assigned to BLM- managed public lands in the Record of Decision for a Resource Management Plan. They are determined by applying management constraints to Visual Resource Inventory Classes.

SOURCE: The various classes are determined for each area of public land according to alternatives and decisions considered in the land use planning process. The Record of Decision documents the applicable locations and classes for management.

DATA FEATURE TYPE: Polygon

THEME TYPE: Generated

HISTORIC RECORD: Yes

UNIQUE IDENTIFIER: Identify by State/Field Office/polygon number. For example, ut050.010 means Utah/Richfield Field Office/polygon #10.

SCALE: 1:100,000

ATTRIBUTES:	CODES:
VRM Class I	I
VRM Class II	II
VRM Class III	III
VRM Class IV	IV

ATTRIBUTE DEFINITIONS:

VRM Class I areas are where only natural ecological changes and very limited management activities are allowed. Any contrast created within the characteristic landscape must not attract attention. This classification is applied to wilderness areas, visual ACEC's, and other similar situations.

VRM Class II areas are where changes in any of the basic elements (form, line, color, texture) caused by a surface-disturbing activity should not be evident in the characteristic landscape. Contrasts must not attract attention.

VRM Class III areas are where contrasts to the basic elements caused by a management activity may be evident, but should remain subordinate to the existing landscape.

VRM Class IV areas are where contrasts may attract attention and be a dominant feature of the landscape in terms of scale, but should repeat the form, line, color, and texture of the characteristic landscape.

Appendix B

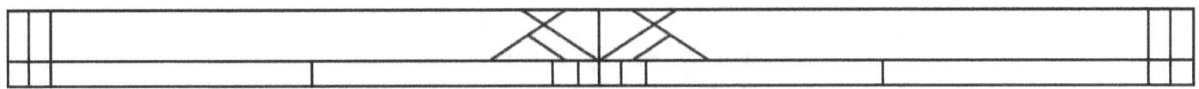

SCENIC QUALITY INVENTORY AND EVALUATION CHART
FROM BLM MANUAL HANDBOOK 8410-1
(Illustration 2)

Illustration 2 - Scenic Quality Inventory and Evaluation Chart

Key factors	Rating Criteria and Score		
Landform	High vertical relief as expressed in prominent cliffs, spires, or massive rock outcrops, or severe surface variation or highly eroded formations including major badlands or dune systems; or detail features dominant and exceptionally striking and intriguing such as glaciers. 5	Steep canyons, mesas, buttes, cinder cones, and drumlins; or interesting erosional patterns or variety in size and shape of landforms; or detail features which are interesting though not dominant or exceptional. 3	Low rolling hills, foothills, or flat valley bottoms; or few or no interesting landscape features. 1
Vegetation	A variety of vegetative types as expressed in interesting forms, textures, and patterns. 5	Some variety of vegetation, but only one or two major types. 3	Little or no variety or contrast in vegetation. 1
Water	Clear and clean appearing, still, or cascading white water, any of which are a dominant factor in the landscape. 5	Flowing, or still, but not dominant in the landscape. 3	Absent, or present, but not noticeable. 0
Color	Rich color combinations, variety or vivid color; or pleasing contrasts in the soil, rock, vegetation, water or snow fields. 5	Some intensity or variety in colors and contrast of the soil, rock and vegetation, but not a dominant scenic element. 3	Subtle color variations, contrast, or interest; generally mute tones. 1
Influence of adjacent scenery	Adjacent scenery greatly enhances visual quality. 5	Adjacent scenery moderately enhances overall visual quality. 3	Adjacent scenery has little or no influence on overall visual quality. 0
Scarcity	One of a kind; or unusually memorable, or very rare within region. Consistent chance for exceptional wildlife or wildflower viewing, etc. * 5+	Distinctive, though somewhat similar to others within the region. 3	Interesting within its setting, but fairly common within the region. 1
Cultural modifications	Modifications add favorably to visual variety while promoting visual harmony. 2	Modifications add little or no visual variety to the area, and introduce no discordant elements. 0	Modifications add variety but are very discordant and promote strong disharmony. -4

* A rating of greater than 5 can be given but must be supported by written justification.

INSTRUCTIONS

Purpose: To rate the visual quality of the scenic resource on all BLM managed lands.

How to Identify Scenic Value: All Bureau lands have scenic value.

How to Determine Minimum Suitability: All BLM lands are rated for scenic values. Also rate adjacent or intermingling non-BLM lands within the planning unit.

When to Evaluate Scenic Quality: Rate for scenery under the most critical conditions (i.e., highest user period or season of use, sidelight, proper atmospheric conditions, etc.).

How to Delineate Rating Areas: Consider the following factors when delineating rating areas.

- 1 Like physiographic characteristics (i.e., land form, vegetation, etc.).

- 2 Similar visual patterns, texture, color, variety, etc.

- 3 Areas which have a similar impact from cultural modifications (i.e., roads, historical and other structures, mining operations, or other surface disturbances).

Explanation of Criteria: (See Illustration 1)

NOTE: Values for each rating criteria are maximum and minimum scores only. It is also possible to assign scores within these ranges.

SCENIC QUALITY
A = 19 or more
B = 12-18
C = 11 or less

Appendix C

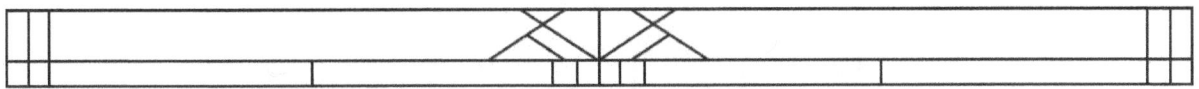

**DETERMING VISUAL RESOURCE INVENTORY CLASSES
FROM BLM MANUAL HANDBOOK 8410-1**
(Illustration 11)

Illustration 11 - Determining Visual Resource Inventory Classes

A. Basis for Determining Visual Resource Inventory Classes

1. Class I. Class I is assigned to all special areas where the current management situations requires maintaining a natural environment essentially unaltered by man.

2. Classes II, III, and IV. These classes are assigned based on combinations of scenic quality, sensitivity levels, and distance zones as shown in the following matrix:

		High			Medium			Low
Special Areas		I	I	I	I	I	I	I
Scenic Quality	**A**	II	II	II	II	II	II	II
	B	II	III	III/IV*	III	IV	IV	IV
	C	III	IV	IV	IV	IV	IV	IV
		f/m	b	s/s	f/m	b	s/s	s/s

Visual Sensitivity Levels (column group header)

Distance Zones (bottom header)

* if adjacent area is Class III or lower, (ie - Class II) assign Class III, if higher, (ie. Class IV) Class IV

B. How to Map Visual Resource Inventory Classes II, III, and IV.

Mapping inventory classes can be cumbersome and time consuming if not done in a systematic manner. Many systems have been developed to do this task. One that has been used effectively is:

Step I: Code each of the 3 overlays as follows:

Scenic Quality	A		B		C	
Sensitivity Levels	High		Medium		Low	
Distance Zones	F/M		B		S/S	

Step 2: Copy the codes from the overlays onto a single new overlay.

Step 3: Delineate the boundaries of the inventory classes on a new overlay using the following information as a guide:

Class II	4 or more lines	
Class III	3 lines	
Class IV	2 lines or less	

REPORT DOCUMENTATION PAGE

Form Approved
OMB No. 0704-0188

Public reporting burden for this collection of information is estimated to average 1 hour per response, including the time for reviewing instructions, searching existing data sources, gathering and maintaining the data needed, and completing and reviewing the collection of information. Send comments regarding this burden estimate or any other aspect of this collection of information, including suggestions for reducing this burden, to Washington Headquarters Services, Directorate for Information Operations and Reports, 1215 Jefferson Davis Highway, Suite 1204, Arlington, VA 22202-4302, and to the Office of Management and Budget, Paperwork Reduction Project (0704-0188), Washington, DC 20503.

1. AGENCY USE ONLY (Leave blank)	2. REPORT DATE	3. REPORT TYPE AND DATES COVERED
		Final

4. TITLE AND SUBTITLE

Integrating GIS Technologies with the Visual Resource Management Inventory Process - Technical Note 407

5. FUNDING NUMBERS

6. AUTHOR(S)

Russell Jackson, Chris Horyza

7. PERFORMING ORGANIZATION NAME(S) AND ADDRESS(ES)

U.S. Department of the Interior
Bureau of Land Management
National Science and Technology Center
P.O. Box 25047
Denver, CO 80225-0047

8. PERFORMING ORGANIZATION REPORT NUMBER

BLM/WO/ST-01/001+8400

9. SPONSORING/MONITORING AGENCY NAME(S) AND ADDRESS(ES)

10. SPONSORING/MONITORING AGENCY REPORT NUMBER

11. SUPPLEMENTARY NOTES

12a. DISTRIBUTION/AVAILABILITY STATEMENT

12b. DISTRIBUTION CODE

13. ABSTRACT (Maximum 200 words)

The purpose of the technical note is to assist BLM field offices in using current geographic information systems (GIS) and image processing technologies to facilitate new, or improve on existing, visual resource management (VRM) inventories. This technical note seeks to use technology available in the field to improve existing VRM inventory procedures without changing the basic concepts the inventory is built on.

Technical Note 407 attempts to modernize the VRM inventory process by taking advantage of advances in GIS and image processing technologies to: enhance the repeatability of VRM results; reduce the amount of time needed to conduct an inventory; reduce the workload that a VRM inventory has on the local office; reduce the cost of the inventory; and improve the quality of VRM inventories for land management decision makers.

14. SUBJECT TERMS

Visual Resource Management Inventory Process, Geographic Information Systems, Image Processing Technologies, VRM Inventory Components.

15. NUMBER OF PAGES

36 including covers

16. PRICE CODE

17. SECURITY CLASSIFICATION OF REPORT	18. SECURITY CLASSIFICATION OF THIS PAGE	19. SECURITY CLASSIFICATION OF ABSTRACT	20. LIMITATION OF ABSTRACT
Unclassified	Unclassified	Unclassified	UL